Celebrating the New Year

written by Traci Sorell

Pearson Education, Inc. 330 Hudson Street, New York, NY 10013

Photo locators denoted as follows Top (T), Center (C), Bottom (B), Left (L), Right (R),
Background (Bkgd)

Cover Aaron Huang/Shutterstock; Back Cover Sorratorn Phosida/Shutterstock.

1 (T) Alexokokok/Shutterstock, (B) Aaron Huang/Shutterstock; 4 Tim Ireland/Xinhua/
Alamy; 6 Aneese/Getty Images; 7 Anouchkia/E+/Getty Images; 13 Unpict/Getty
Images; 17 istockphoto/Getty Images; 18 (T) Blue Jean Images/Alamy, (B) photo26/
Getty Images; 19 (T) LeeYiuTung/Getty Images, (B) Sorratorn Phosida/Shutterstock;
20 Marco Saroldi/Alamy; 21 Szefei Wong/Alamy; 22 Aaron Huang/Shutterstock; 23
(T) MarcelClemens/Shutterstock, (C) mtphoto19/Alamy Stock Photo; 24 EuroStyle
Graphics/Alamy.

ISBN-13: 978-0-328-94186-5
ISBN-10:   0-328-94186-7
4 19

Table of Contents

Happy New Year!

Around the world, many people celebrate the New Year. Some people celebrate with big parades and fireworks. Others have quieter celebrations. They gather with family. They share special meals. In some places, people race around with empty suitcases! Others eat fruit as fast as they can.

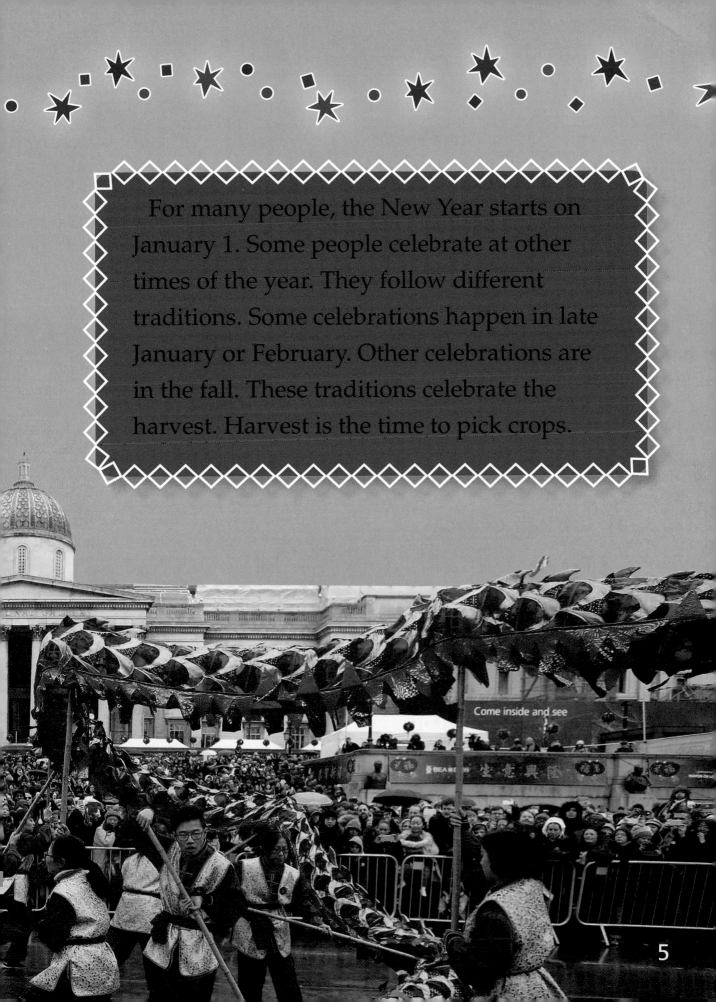

For many people, the New Year starts on January 1. Some people celebrate at other times of the year. They follow different traditions. Some celebrations happen in late January or February. Other celebrations are in the fall. These traditions celebrate the harvest. Harvest is the time to pick crops.

Outdoor Parties

In the United States, New Year's Day is on January 1. People begin celebrating the night before on New Year's Eve. Some cities have big outdoor parties. Families watch parades. Fireworks light up the sky.

Fireworks in Dallas, Texas

Confetti falling in New York City

One of the biggest New Year's parties is in New York City. Thousands come to hear music and to dance. They cheer as a large glass ball glides down a tall pole. Colorful paper confetti rains down on the happy crowd.

Feasts, Dancing, and Face Painting

In Canada and Mexico, many people celebrate on January 1. The Nisga'a are a native group in Canada. They welcome the New Year early in February, on a night with a crescent moon. This sliver of moon is a sign of a good harvest. People feast and dance.

A Nisga'a New Year's celebration

The Seri nation in Mexico welcomes the New Year in summer. Summer is when new crops begin to grow. The people paint their faces. They dance. They sing traditional songs. They thank the sun and moon for bringing light and life to Earth for one more year.

Seri face painting

Suitcases and Skipping over Waves

New Year's Day for most South Americans is January 1. Some countries have unusual ways to celebrate. In Colombia, people run around with empty suitcases. They believe this tradition will bring travel in the New Year.

In Brazil, people dress in all-white clothing. They enjoy picnics on the beach. At midnight, they jump into the water. They try to skip over seven waves. They hope this tradition will bring them good luck in the New Year.

Fun with Food

In Spain, people race against time. The race happens at midnight on December 31. At that hour, clocks chime 12 times. People eat a grape for each chime. They eat 12 grapes. Many people start the New Year with a mouth full of grapes!

Eating grapes at midnight in Spain

In Switzerland, some people drop a scoop of ice cream on the floor! The falling ice cream is a symbol of overflowing good luck. They hope this tradition will bring good luck for the next 12 months.

Celebrating Nature

In Ethiopia, New Year's celebrations focus on nature. For many people, the New Year begins in September. Young girls dress in traditional clothing. They sing special songs. They pick flowers as gifts for friends. In return, the friends give them gifts of money.

Giving flowers for Enkutatash

This celebration is called Enkutatash. It means "gift of jewels." The celebration comes at the end of a long rainy season. The weather becomes bright and sunny. Beautiful daisies cover the countryside like yellow jewels. These are the flowers that children give as gifts.

Making New Year's Resolutions

Boys march in a New Year's celebration in Egypt.

Many people around the world make New Year's resolutions. A resolution is like a promise to do better in the New Year. Some sources say that the first people to make resolutions were in the Middle East. The tradition may have started in Babylon 4,000 years ago. Babylon was a city in what is now the country of Iraq. Today, people in many Arab-speaking countries celebrate the New Year at different times. Many of these people make resolutions for the New Year.

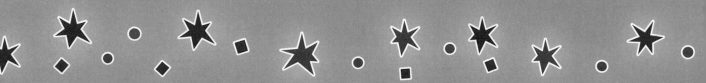

In Israel, people welcome the New Year in early fall. They think about the past year. They think about changes they could make in the New Year. They make resolutions. Families gather and share special foods. Honey and apples stand for sweet success in the New Year. Eating a pomegranate symbolizes hope for good fortune in the coming year.

Families in Israel celebrate with a meal of special foods.

Family Time and Festive Parades

In China, New Year's Day happens between January and February. It is called Lunar New Year. Families eat big dinners. They honor family members from the past. People give each other money in red envelopes. Red is for good luck.

Other countries in Asia celebrate Lunar New Year too. People who march in parades wear colorful costumes. Bright lanterns and red banners decorate the streets. People perform a dragon dance. They hope the dance will bring good luck.

Beautiful Drawings and Flickering Lamps

Some people in India mark their New Year in April. They celebrate the beginning of the growing season. Farmers prepare the earth for new crops. Women make beautiful drawings on the ground. They call the drawings *kolam*. Families also eat special foods. They make many dishes with mangoes.

A kolam drawing

Other people in India celebrate with the Festival of Lights. The celebration lasts five days each fall. People decorate their homes with lamps. Families gather to visit and give gifts. They wear new clothes. Long ago, the festival marked the last harvest of the year.

Fireworks, Stars, and Kites

Australia celebrates the New Year on January 1. In the city of Sydney, boats fill the harbor on New Year's Eve. People line up along the water's edge. They cheer as fireworks explode and light up the sky over the famous Sydney Harbor Bridge.

The Maori are native people who live in New Zealand. They mark the New Year in spring. They watch the night sky for a special group of stars that appear only at this time of year. The community celebrates with a great feast. They also fly giant, colorful kites. Some kites are as long as 98 feet (30 meters). That's about as long as three school buses end to end!

People around the world celebrate the New Year in many ways. Some have parties. Some think about the past year or make wishes for the year to come. A new year brings hope and excitement. That is always something to celebrate!